TOURETTE SYNDROME

TOURETTE SYNDROME

WITHDRAWN

MARLENE TARG BRILL

 Twenty-First Century Books • Minneapolis

Many people helped me gather information and prepare this book.
I wish to thank Carol Blustein, Tourette Syndrome Association of Illinois;
and Iris Gimble, speech pathologist, for pointing me in the right direction
to locate resources and contact people to interview; and Sue Levi-Pearl,
Tourette Syndrome Association, for the thoughtful reading of the manuscript.
A special thank you goes to all the caring families who shared their
stories so others can understand TS better.

Photographs courtesy of AP/Wide World Photos: p. 15; © Lowell Handler: pp.
19, 21, 25, 47, 71; © Bettmann/Corbis: p. 39; Photo Researchers, Inc.: pp. 53
(© Mark C. Burnett/Science Source), 61 (© Will & Deni McIntyre), 77 (© Joseph
Szabo), 92 (© Ulrike Welsch); PhotoEdit: pp. 57 (© Robert Brenner), 69 (© Tony
Freeman), 82 (© Tony Freeman), 89 (© Tony Freeman); Visuals Unlimited: p. 59
(© Nancy P. Alexander); © SuperStock: p. 87

Twenty-First Century Books
A division of Lerner Publishing Group
241 First Avenue North
Minneapolis, MN 55401 U.S.A.

Website address: www.lernerbooks.com

Library of Congress Cataloging-in-Publication Data

Brill, Marlene Targ.
Tourette syndrome / Marlene Targ Brill.
p. cm. (Twenty-first century medical library)
Includes bibliographical references and index.
Summary: Examines the tic disorder known as Tourette syndrome, its symptoms
and manifestations, how it can be controlled and treated, and, through case
studies, what it is like to live with Tourette's.
ISBN: 0-7613-2101-2 (lib. bdg.)
1. Tourette syndrome—Juvenile literature. 2. Tourette syndrome—Case studies—
Juvenile literature. 3. Tourette syndrome in children—Juvenile literature. [1.
Tourette syndrome. 2. Tic disorders.]
RC375 .B75 2002   2001041747

Manufactured in the United States of America
2 3 4 5 6 7 – BP – 10 09 08 07 06 05

CONTENTS

TOURETTE SYNDROME

Chapter One

THE MANY FACES OF TOURETTE SYNDROME

Raymond's Story

Out of nowhere, Raymond started to sniff and click his tongue when he was five. Thinking something was wrong, his parents took him to the doctor, who gave him allergy tests and medication. When the sniffing continued, another doctor decided he had a hole in his nose and operated. But Raymond kept sniffing. Without clear-cut answers, his mother insisted he sniffed on purpose to annoy her. She yelled at him to stop.

Then Raymond began licking his arm. Jerking his head, blinking his eyes, and, more embarrassing, grabbing his genitals, followed. After another round of doctor's visits, Raymond heard that he had Tourette syndrome (TS). By this time he was ten years old, and other kids noticed how he acted.

9

"I would get teased constantly," Raymond remembered at age seventeen. *"I had a real bad time. People wouldn't even ask why I was doing these things. They just made fun of me. Some seemed scared. I'd hear them talking about me behind my back. A lot of times I cried. And I acted out and hit kids."*

Symptoms changed as Raymond got older. His hands and toes jerked, and his fingers tapped on desks and tabletops. He repeated phrases other people said. Unusual mouth sounds came and went. Although normally a good student, in junior high Raymond found organizing his work more difficult. He seemed to lose the ability to set priorities. He never did his homework. He became unusually anxious in stressful situations and couldn't concentrate. Test-taking triggered grunts and smacking noises, which bothered classmates who needed quiet to think.

In seventh grade, Raymond developed habits he could not break. His TS symptoms now included certain compulsions, actions he had to perform. At home, he asked questions, even when he already knew the answers. At school, he raised his hand in class whether or not he had an answer or question. Raymond could figure out problems by himself, but he needed to ask questions that others found obvious. Teachers thought he took up too much class time. Classmates found him weird and made fun of him. Throughout junior high school, he had almost no friends.

However, everything improved for Raymond in high school. The school counselor helped him learn to organize his time better. He was allowed to take tests in another room or without time limits on days his sounds or movements interfered with working. Raymond's grades, especially in math, soared. Finding friends who wouldn't make fun of him, however, made the biggest difference. Gradually, Raymond gained confidence. He joined the school soccer team and ran track off-season. He still jerked his head sometimes or made strange sounds, but he learned to mask these movements to look more natural. For example, he sat on his hand in class when the urge to ask an unnecessary question hit. Some tics, like rubbing his crotch, went away, only to be replaced by leg shaking. His main problem became controlling his body's need to repeat certain movements, like drinking water from every fountain he passed. As his grades remained high and he felt less stress about schoolwork, Raymond realized he had a shot at a good college to train as an engineer.

Caroline's Story

Caroline first noticed her symptoms in second grade. Her head jolted sideways as if she were flicking bangs off her face. Then throat clearing began. Her sisters screamed at her to stop the irritating sounds. At first, her parents told her to stop, too. As the sounds continued, however, they worried something awful was happening to their daughter.

Caroline's mother dragged her to a string of doctors. The first one thought Caroline had allergies. He gave her tests and medication and later shots, believing a nasal drip caused the throat clearing. Still, the sounds continued. After several more tests from doctors who never discovered the problem, Caroline's family doctor suggested that she might have Tourette syndrome. This doctor changed her medication, but the new medicine made her sleepy. When the movements worsened, the doctor upped her dose of medicine, which made her sleepier. Within a few months, Caroline faced another problem: Being tired often worsened unwanted movements. Caroline discovered that controlling her movements by taking pills was a constant balancing act to find the right medication and correct dosage.

Not satisfied with her daughter's progress, Caroline's mother gave her vitamins, food supplements, and special diets. Nothing prevented the changing parade of symptoms that assaulted Caroline's body. Her jaw twisted until it ached. Her teeth chomped down on the inside of her cheeks until the skin swelled. In eighth grade, she produced a series of noticeable clicking noises. Most often, they occurred when everyone was quiet, such as during tests. Head jerks and mouth movements, which she found equally embarrassing, came out more at dances or mixers. By now, a few classmates made fun of her movements. Caroline never spoke about having TS, but others could see she was having a rough time.

"It makes me really mad when my tics become noticeable," Caroline, now sixteen, grumbled. "I feel like the odd person, different from everybody."

By high school, many of the painful combinations of twists and jerks faded. Medication still made her sleepy, but it never affected her good grades. Although having Tourette syndrome sometimes made her angry, she realized this was part of who she was. She began telling close friends that she had TS. Little by little, she accepted the strange movements that were beyond her control.

Brian's Story

Brian's mother first noticed her son's unusual behavior when he was eight weeks old. She saw odd rhythmic patterns in her baby's arm and leg movements. Within a short time, Brian added eye blinking and low-pitched droning sounds to his wild movements.

By age four, he showed promise of being unusually bright. He held conversations like a much older child. He read books. But he alternated between sitting for hours reading and becoming a bundle of uncontrollable activity. His flailing legs narrowly missed knocking over furniture, and his side-to-side head rolling on the rough carpet rubbed a bald spot on the back of his head.

One day Brian started rhythmic jumping. After his mother scolded him several times to stop, he said, "I heard you, but my brain is telling me to jump and hum, and it talks louder than you do."[1]

Brian's mother knew something was wrong. Yet doctors told her she was too anxious. She had the problem, not her son. To make matters worse, Brian's movements came and went. By the time she arranged a doctor's appointment, any signs of a problem were gone, adding to the difficulty of discovering what caused Brian's actions.

In school, Brian was a study in contrasts. He read Pippi Longstocking *at age six and Stephen King books by age eight. He imitated voices and memorized the entire musical score of* Cats, *but he could not remember multiplication tables. He was a good athlete, yet hand tremors turned his writing into unreadable chicken scratchings, and he struggled to hit the correct computer keys. Brian was nine when his mother stumbled upon an article that best described him. It was about Tourette syndrome. Armed with this new evidence, she found a doctor who finally agreed with the diagnosis.*

Brian was lucky in that he always had friends. His keen sense of humor, funny voices, and acting talent attracted other kids. He also projected an attitude of "If you tease me, I'm going to punch out your lights."

At home, however, Brian had a temper. From age twelve to seventeen, he never went a day without becoming angry at someone. Situations that seemed unimportant to others caused violent outbursts in Brian. On several occasions, he smashed through the closed glass storm door. For years, his brother feared being alone with him. Brian hated how quick he was to anger and felt sorry after his temper flared. He was convinced he was evil.

Medication and time helped tame the storm inside Brian. He completed high school, but he had trouble holding a job and finishing the college acting classes he loved. He once left a job

PEOPLE WITH TOURETTE SYNDROME

- Calvin Peete, professional golfer who won twelve titles in seven seasons
- Jim Eisenreich, former major league ballplayer
- Mahmoud Abdul-Rauf, star basketball guard with the Denver Nuggets
- Samuel Johnson (1709–1784), author of the first English dictionary, thought to have had TS
- Gary James Marmer, physicist with Argonne National Laboratory and author
- Mike Higgins, former U.S. Army captain
- Wolfgang Amadeus Mozart (1756–1791), Austrian composer and pianist, thought to have had TS
- Michael Wolff, pianist and jazz musician
- Lowell Handler, photographer and author

Basketball star Mahmoud Abdul-Rauf, center

because his trembling hands couldn't open the lock on his locker. Rather than tell his boss, he quit. Another problem was the panic attacks that now accompanied his TS. He never panicked on stage, but groundless fears kept him from entering the school building or classroom. Still, at age twenty-four Brian refused to give up. He wrote at home where he felt safe, with his mother typing his work. He hoped that one day he could go back to college, perhaps to become a professional author, actor, or director.

Like many people, Brian, Caroline, and Raymond never heard of Tourette syndrome before their doctors and parents explained their disorder to them. Yet thousands of children receive this diagnosis each year. Researchers estimate that severe TS affects more than 100,000 people in the United States alone. About one in two hundred Americans find they have very mild signs of TS. Countless others struggle through life feeling something is wrong with them but never learning what it is. And those around them wonder whether their jumpy friends and neighbors are safe to be near.

Part of the TS puzzle is the broad range of symptoms, from barely noticeable to severe and life-altering. Some symptoms appear as occasional jerks or grimaces. Others involve uncontrollable spasms and shouts that can be disabling. Because of these unexpected and uncommon behaviors, a person with TS is often viewed as an oddity, someone to tease or fear. Too many children with TS go through endless tortures in and out of school because they refuse to tell anyone or, if they do, classmates are unable to understand their condition.

One way to build understanding, combat prejudice, and open factual discussions about Tourette syndrome is to learn more about this curious disorder. Perhaps you know someone like Caroline or Brian. Perhaps you are like Raymond or some of the other people you will meet later in this book. Either way, this book is for you and those who are close to you—your friends, family, and classmates.

Chapter Two

WHAT IS TOURETTE SYNDROME?

[Tourette syndrome] is like having poison ivy all over your body, for twenty years, and constantly being told not to scratch. You can resist for a while, but eventually you give in. [1]

TICS

Tourette syndrome is a physical disorder. People who have it make movements and sounds, called *tics*, that are beyond their control. When a tic occurs, the brain tells one or more muscles to contract, which causes the unwanted sounds or movements. These movements seem to happen without a particular purpose. They come on suddenly and quickly and repeat without warning.

Twitchy Tics

Tics may affect any part of the body at any time. *Vocal tics* originate in the muscles that control speech. A range of sudden sounds may include anything from smacking, hissing, and throat clearing to shouts of words or phrases. *Motor tics* can occur in any muscles of the body, producing various movements from eye blinking and nose wrinkling to leg jerks, hops, and arm thrusts.

A vocal tic in progress. This young woman makes screeching sounds.

Symptoms and their severity differ widely among various people. Tics can be mild or severe or somewhere in the middle. Not all people with TS exhibit all symptoms. How much TS affects specific behaviors depends on each person's special physical makeup. One or more tics can occur several times a minute or only a few times a day or week. Certain tics may remain in some form throughout a lifetime. Others may appear elsewhere in the body or change into milder or more severe forms. Some tics, such as temper outbursts, may fade completely with time.

Simple and Complex Tics

Doctors define tics as simple or complex, depending on the number of involved body parts. Individual movements of only one body part, such as shoulder shrugging or head jerking, are called *simple tics*. Similarly, individual sounds, such as sniffing and grunting, that are produced by forcing air through either the nose, throat, or vocal cords are simple vocal tics.

Complex tics involve several muscle groups that trigger patterns of movements. Examples of complex motor tics are picking scabs or jumping. More embarrassing tics involve other people, such as touching someone else, imitating others' actions (*echopraxia),* and making offensive gestures (*copropraxia*).

Complex vocal tics include *echolalia*, *palilalia*, and *coprolalia*. With echolalia, a person repeats the last sound, word, or phrase said by someone else. For example, after a father says, "Clean your room," his son may repeat, "Clean your room." With palilalia, the boy may repeat his own words or sounds, saying, "I'll clean my room, room, room" or "I'll clean my room-m-m-m."

The most well-known symptom of TS is coprolalia, cursing or saying socially inappropriate words or

A complex muscle tic might involve rapid arm movements like those experienced by this young artist and sculptor.

phrases for a given culture. When television shows and movies feature people with TS, they often choose someone who lets out a string of swear words or sexual terms for no apparent reason. Therefore, many people assume that anyone who tics also swears, which is untrue. Less than 15 percent of individuals with TS struggle with coprolalia.

COMMON MOTOR AND VOCAL TICS

Motor Tics

simple:

eye blinking
leg jerking
head jerking
neck twisting
finger moving
tongue thrusting
shoulder shrugging
muscle tensing
nose wrinkling
toe bending

complex:

forming unusual faces
touching other people or
   things
leaping
twirling
biting, hitting, rubbing, or
   other self- destructive
   actions
smelling objects
imitating others' actions
   (echopraxia)
making offensive gestures
   (copropraxia)

Vocal Tics

simple:

sniffing
grunting
throat clearing
lip smacking
belching
hissing
tongue clicking
coughing
yelping
barking

complex:

saying words or phrases
   out of context
producing animal sounds
repeating a sound, word,
   or phrase someone
   else just said (echolalia)
repeating one's own words
   or sounds (palilalia)
saying offensive words or
   phrases (coprolalia)
spitting
stuttering

One mother found this knowledge comforting: "I didn't understand that many more people have mild TS than severe," she said. "When my son was first diagnosed, I was so freaked out. Then my doctor explained that TS has a range of symptoms. That was such a relief to me to learn what a small percentage swearing is."

Suppressing Tics

Most children with TS begin ticcing between three and ten years old. The first signs are commonly eye blinking or throat clearing, although any kind of tic can develop. Different tics may soon follow. Without proper diagnosis, these children are unsure what is happening to their seemingly out-of-control body.

By early adolescence (between nine and thirteen years), tics may worsen. One reason involves the change in hormones. Another stems from the normal concern many teenagers have about their maturing bodies and what others think about them. Worry only adds to the stress of dealing with TS.

The concern about body image has its upside. Like any teen, those with TS gain greater awareness of their body as they mature. Now they may *feel* the sudden urge to tic a split second before it happens. With this information, many teens learn to identify what triggers their tics and how to better handle them in different situations. Although tics never fully go away, people who have them gain some control over when and where they happen.

Many, but not all, people say they can suppress their tics. Some claim to hold back tics for up to thirty minutes or an hour. This allows them time to find a private place to let the tics out. Like a sneeze or hiccup, tics need to be expressed eventually. Trying to hold them in only creates tension inside the body that must be released. Often, delayed tics explode with greater force and last longer than the original urge to tic.

"It's like a ball of energy that builds, like having to go to the bathroom. Eventually, you have to go," Brian explains. "This massive amount of energy has to come out. For me, I can hold it to a certain point. Then I know I have to go someplace private and let a couple loose. Then there is this sense of relief. I feel less anxious."

Reducing Tics

Many people with TS report that their tics lessen during periods of exercise. Rhythmic physical activity seems to refocus the energy needed to produce tics. Similarly, tics may disappear while concentrating on an absorbing activity, such as listening to music, reading, or drawing.

Famous neurologist and author Oliver Sacks saw firsthand how focusing eases tics. He followed a surgeon with TS through his daily routine to understand how he could perform such delicate work. The doctor told Sacks that at home he sometimes flung objects—an iron, a rolling pin, saucepans—as if enraged and had compulsions to do everything in threes or fives. At the hospital, Sacks watched in amazement as the doctor

Dr. Oliver Sacks is the neurologist and author whose clinical experiences and writings inspired the film *Awakenings*.

walked down hallways skipping at each fifth step. Suddenly, he would reach for the ground as if he were scooping up something. In meetings, he tapped coworkers and occasionally rolled on his side to touch their shoulders with his toes. What fascinated Sacks most, however, was the doctor's ability to handle surgery despite all this darting and touching. "B. took the knife, made a bold, clear incision—there was no hint of any ticcing or distraction," Sacks wrote. [2]

DIAGNOSING TOURETTE SYNDROME

Not everyone who tics has Tourette syndrome. Diseases of the nervous system and long-term use of certain mind-altering drugs can cause tics but not TS. A blow to the head, such as from a car accident, can injure the brain and leave someone with tics.

Then there is the normal range of childhood tics that appear and disappear by themselves as the nervous system develops. One in five children experiences some kind of tic for a few months or a year during childhood, especially when nervous or under stress, such as during a test. These tics are usually mild and hardly noticeable. Even tics that are visible rarely interfere with everyday activities enough to cause concern.

Tics that last for over a year or are so severe that they disrupt school or play may be related to Tourette syndrome. Physicians confirm the diagnosis of TS after observing symptoms and ruling out other health conditions with blood tests and body scans. A case history is taken from the patient and parents, who describe their child's behavior and family history. If no other problems surface, doctors follow guidelines for TS set by the American Psychiatric Association. According to these guidelines, physicians look for:

- both multiple motor tics and at least one vocal tic
- tics that last a year without a tic-free period of more than three straight months
- symptoms that begin before age eighteen

Even with these guidelines, making a diagnosis can be tricky. The exact cause of TS remains unknown. That is why TS is called a *syndrome* rather than a disease. A disease, such as measles or chicken pox, has known causes and definite signs that signal what it is. With a syndrome, however, there are no blood tests or body scans to prove it exists. A syndrome is merely a collection of observed symptoms that have been given a name. Therefore, diagnosis is made largely by observing and reporting.

"My first symptoms appeared at age six," Mark, age thirty-seven, remembers. "I bit my lip. My parents thought I had a speech problem, so I was off to a speech pathologist. Other than not pronouncing my S's and P's, she couldn't find anything wrong. Thinking the biting was a mental health issue, she suggested sending me to a psychologist. Then barking and other noises and movements started. Five years later I got diagnosed only because my parents read about someone in the paper and tracked down the doctor who had diagnosed the person."

Years ago, families went from doctor to doctor because so few recognized the symptoms. Five to ten years of searching and worrying were common. Today, doctors are better able to recognize signs of TS. Some patients receive their diagnosis within six months to a year after consulting with a doctor about their symptoms. The media, too, are beginning to show the kinder, more normal side of TS, thereby encouraging the public to become more accepting of people with TS. With more positive and correct information available, people who cope with tics are seeking diagnosis and treatment sooner.

OVERLAPPING DISORDERS

Diagnosis becomes complicated when symptoms of TS appear in combination with other conditions. A wide spectrum of behaviors overlaps or mimics other disorders, some much more disabling than TS. However, not all people with a TS diagnosis struggle with these other disorders. Yet those with TS have a greater likelihood of also having something else.

Many of these disorders share common symptoms. In fact, researchers suspect that these conditions may stem from related causes. Tics may be the most visible sign for most people with TS. Many are also obsessive, compulsive, unable to attend, hyperactive, impulsive, disorganized, or depressed, or experience sleep, mood, and learning problems (Fig 2.1).

Obsessive-Compulsive Disorder (OCD)

About 33 percent of children who tic exhibit obsessions and compulsions. *Obsessions* are thoughts or images that return over and over again. A person with an obsession can be compared to a child who is stuck on the same bedtime story. In the worst case, obsessions interfere with daily functions so often that they leave the person feeling upset and out of control. For example, some people worry that dirt and germs will infect their body, or they fear harm or sickness will come to themselves or family members. Everything they do revolves around keeping safe and free of disease. People with uncommon worries may also be consumed

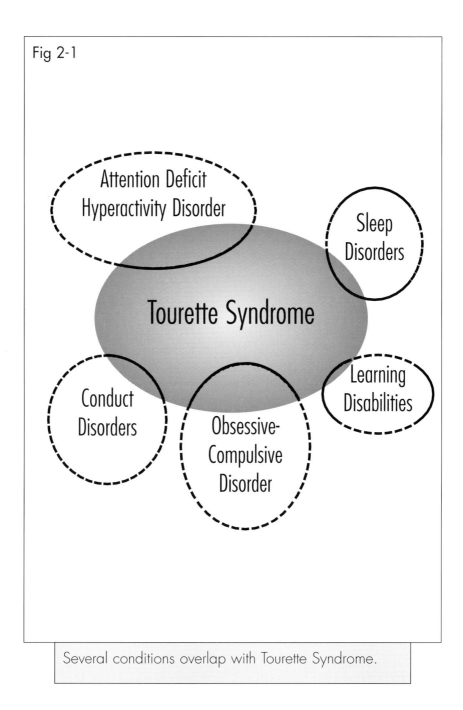

Fig 2-1

Attention Deficit
Hyperactivity Disorder

Sleep
Disorders

Tourette Syndrome

Conduct
Disorders

Obsessive-
Compulsive
Disorder

Learning
Disabilities

Several conditions overlap with Tourette Syndrome.

with thoughts about certain words, objects, or numbers, or need things arranged a certain way. Worries and superstitions are part of everyday life. But for someone who is truly obsessed, these uncomfortable feelings bring extreme fear, sickness, or doubt.

A few people complain that their mind races with these thoughts. This interferes with sleep, speech, and daily activities. One mother remembers her teenager as a young child:

"My son had many thoughts racing through his mind, so he had trouble expressing himself. The thoughts were not always related to what we were talking about at the time or what he wanted to say, so we were always trying to make connections to why he was saying something. Part of his frustration was we couldn't understand what he was saying."

Compulsions are what obsessive people do to make their discomfort go away. Compulsions are actions that must be performed repeatedly according to rules defined by the particular obsession. For example, those who fear germs may wash their hands until the skin cracks, or they may touch the doorknob a certain number of times to keep strangers away. Similarly, a child may feel an overpowering need to hear a song or wear a certain pair of socks, or a student may recheck homework so many times that the deadline for handing it in passes (Fig. 2.2).

These people understand that their obsessions make no sense. Still, they are unable to control the urge to satisfy them. It's as if their brain gets stuck on a particular thought or urge that keeps them from doing anything else. When obsessions and compulsions become this strong, someone is said to have obsessive-compulsive disorder (OCD). People with OCD often say the symptoms feel like a case of mental hiccups that won't go away. [3]

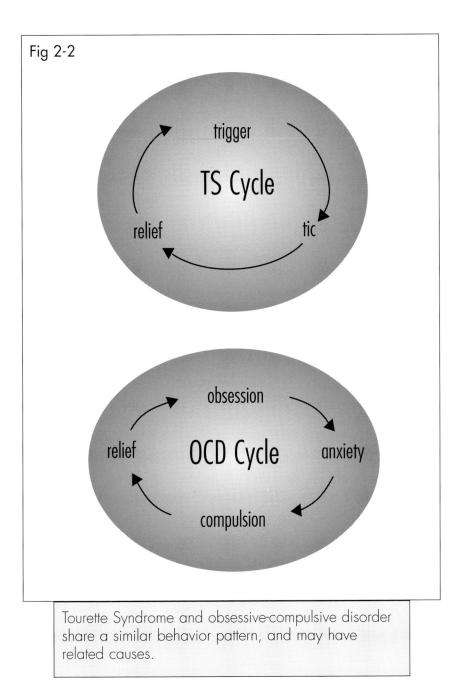

Fig 2-2

trigger

TS Cycle

relief

tic

obsession

relief

OCD Cycle

anxiety

compulsion

Tourette Syndrome and obsessive-compulsive disorder share a similar behavior pattern, and may have related causes.

"Obsession is thinking about something, and a compulsion is doing something," explains Mark, who has OCD traits and TS. "You keep doing it until you get it right. It's like a tic, but when I'm ticcing, I don't even know I'm doing it. With a compulsion, there might be a thought process, like with my touching my nose. I keep thinking about the word 'touch.' The compulsion is I got to do it, I got to do it, I got to do it."

Attention Deficit Disorder With or Without Hyperactivity (ADD or ADHD)

Another common condition that can occur with TS is attention deficit disorder (ADD). Children who have ADD find it difficult to focus attention, control impulses, and behave as expected. They are easily distracted by the slightest sound or movement. They have problems concentrating on what they do and what others say. Unable to stay focused, they lose track of what is going on, leading to endless disorganization. Consequently, they seem forgetful, unable to follow directions, and incapable of completing schoolwork, chores, or projects.

Some children with ADD fidget constantly and talk excessively—blurting out answers before questions are completed and interrupting conversations. Many of these children are also hyperactive (ADHD). Usually, children show signs of being hyper before TS symptoms emerge. Even so, some doctors caution that a few medicines for ADD bring out or worsen tics for people with Tourettes.

Because they cannot attend well, children with ADD and ADHD struggle with relationships. They cannot wait their turn, and they appear never to listen, which drives away friends. Lacking the ability to stop themselves, children with ADHD often take dangerous

COMMON OBSESSIONS AND COMPULSIONS

Obsessions

- suffers unusual worry or doubt
- worries about dirt and germs
- needs order and symmetry
- fears scary or harmful things will happen
- imagines losing control and becoming aggressive
- sees sexual images frequently
- is consumed by moral/religious thoughts
- mentally rearranges letters and words
- fixated on a number or letter

Compulsions

- checks and rechecks continually
- practices washing and cleaning rules
- counts things or tries to even up sides or numbers of things
- touches self, others, objects
- moves or arranges objects by certain number patterns
- arranges and lines up items constantly
- seeks continual approval
- repeats actions
- erases mistakes
- tattles or prays excessively
- hoards and saves

risks without thinking of consequences. As with TS, symptoms of ADD can come and go, causing others to figure that these behaviors can be controlled. Unlike TS, others cannot see the inner storm that influences why and how someone who has ADD or OCD behaves. All three conditions involve problems with the nervous system that are beyond someone's control.

Fourteen-year-old Aaron describes his disorder this way: "I can be really hyper and out of control. I run around making noises—actually sensations that my chest screams. I used to buy things compulsively. I have more energy than most people, which is a good thing about being hyperactive, and I don't tire easily. I could stay up all night if I had a good TV to watch. I don't like having to be up at a certain time, and I hate the mornings. I'm kind of hyper at school, too. I get sent to the principal's office a couple of times a day. I have to say over and over, 'I will follow directions and respect people's property.'"

Learning Disabilities

Tourette syndrome does nothing to change intelligence. But children who have TS may have various learning disabilities. Constant eye blinking and body jerking or poor control can interfere with learning, making reading, concentrating, and writing difficult.

About 30 percent of children with TS have serious learning disabilities in addition to tics. The clearest signs of learning disabilities are low grades and poor performance. Usually, trouble comes from difficulty learning basic skills in reading, spelling, writing, and math. Students with a learning disability are unable to process information they see, hear, or remember in the same way as other students. They try just as hard. But they fail tests and never seem to get good grades. Unable to cope with their schoolwork, they become frustrated. Eventually, they lose interest and stop trying.

"I'm not a good student," Jake, age thirteen, admits. "I have this project that I completely forgot was due this week. I thought it would be easy, but it's not. I hate to study. I hate doing homework. Teachers annoy me. I hate school."

Sleep Disorders

Sleep problems are common among people with TS. Sometimes, tics make falling asleep difficult. Once asleep, people who tic may awaken frequently during the night or walk and talk in their sleep. Sleep studies confirm that some people with TS exhibit motor and vocal tics when they are asleep that are similar to those observed when awake. Others find their tics lessen or disappear during sleep.

"In third grade, Jake's most significant problem was related to sleep," his father remembers. "He was having long periods when you could hear him ticcing in bed, and he would have his action figures under his cover. He banged them together to mask his vocal tics. He still has a lot of sleep problems. It takes him a long time to get to sleep."

Conduct Problems

For unknown reasons, a few people with TS display huge mood swings. Usually, they also have another condition, such as ADD or OCD. For some of them, extreme feelings overwhelm them on a daily, monthly, or yearly basis. Outbursts of rage can far exceed standard temper tantrums and normal personality differences among individuals. These outbursts seem to come out of nowhere with little prompting and explode into wild fury. Once started, rages must follow their course until all energy is gone. One person with TS claims he has a need to see or feel things break or his rage isn't satisfied.[4] These outbursts are not about anger. They are more about having a short fuse and needing to let off steam. Afterward, most people who rage feel ashamed or guilty about what they have done.

"I knew very well how awful it felt to be stuck in a rage that there was no excuse for," Brian explains. "My unrestrained expression of rage was completely disproportionate to the trigger. The horrible part was that I could not get out of it or even indicate in any way (to my targets) that I knew I was being unfair. I could only wait for it to pass. It was as if a cloud of rage had floated by and seized me, filling me up for a while before it drifted off on its way again. Finding out that, for me, rage is a part of my overall symptoms was a great relief in comparison with the years I spent agonizing over my evilness. I was not born bad. I am neither aggressive nor dangerous. Learning the reason was the gift that prompted me to deal with it."

Chapter Three

WHAT CAUSES TOURETTE SYNDROME?

"Madame de D . . . at the age of seven was afflicted by convulsive movements of the hand and arms. . . . After each spasm, the movements of the hand became more regular and better controlled until a convulsive movement would again interrupt her work. . . . As the disease progressed, and the spasms spread to involve her voice and speech, the young lady made strange screams and said words that made no sense. However, during all this, she was clearly alert, and showed no signs of delirium [being confused] or other mental problems. . . .

In the midst of an interesting conversation, all of a sudden, without being able to prevent it, she interrupts what she is saying or what she is listening to with horrible screams and with words that are even more extraordinary than *her screams. All of this contrasts . . . with her distinguished manners and background. These words are, for the most part, offensive curse words and obscene sayings. These are no less embarrassing for her than for those who have to listen, the expressions being so crude that an unfavorable opinion of the woman is almost inevitable." (Jean Marc Itard, 1825)*[1]

LONG HISTORY OF TOURETTE SYNDROME

Tourette syndrome is not new. Ancient Greeks recorded examples of sudden facial movements, barking, and cursing almost two thousand years ago. Since then, physicians from every era have written about individuals who twitched and shouted, never knowing why.

Hundreds of years ago, some people with tics were worshiped or thought enchanted. Many more, however, were considered mentally ill, or tortured, jailed, or burned as witches. One researcher claimed that several women burned during the 1692 Salem witchcraft trials may have displayed signs of Tourette syndrome, clues that confirmed to the townspeople that the women were bewitched. Fortunately, times—and thinking—have changed.

Our modern understanding of TS developed from the writings of French neurologist Jean Marc Itard. In 1825, he described nineteen years of troubling behaviors in one patient, the Marquise de Dampierre, a French noblewoman. As quoted in the chapter opening, Itard wrote that the marquise's problems began with motor tics when she was seven. Soon she added vocal tics that eventually developed into cursing and screams. Although she married, the marquise spent much of her time hidden from polite society. She remained the topic of gossip until her death in 1884 at eighty-six.

The bizarre behavior and verbal outbursts of several young women confounded the Puritan community of Salem, leading to the witch trials of 1692. Recent theories suggest the possibility of Tourette syndrome as a factor.

The year after she died, another French neurologist and former student of Itard's identified nine patients who displayed assorted bursts of movements and sounds. Dr. Georges Gilles de la Tourette compared his patients' tics with the Marquise's strange symptoms and wrote a paper about their similarities. Because he was the first to describe a separate tic disorder, it was called *maladie des tics de Gilles de la Tourette* in his honor.

French neurologist Georges Gilles de la Tourette

Dr. Gilles de la Tourette believed that patients with TS could not control their tics. He further assumed that TS ran in families. He was sure the odd behaviors stemmed from neurological (physical) rather than psychological (emotional) problems.

The twentieth century brought a new wave of thinking about many illnesses, including TS. A few doctors suggested that sudden head movements, throat clearing, and sniffing resulted from sinus and tonsil infections. These doctors removed the infected parts through surgery and, without proper follow-up, declared the patients cured. While many patients probably suffered from infections, those who actually had TS went untreated after their surgery.

A growing interest in psychology and how the mind works led to a different understanding of TS. Now the condition came under the heading of mental illness. *Psychologists* and *psychiatrists* searched for any number of mental causes for the puzzling behaviors displayed in their offices. They claimed patients who ticced were mad or unstable. They figured some terrible secret from the patient's life was being expressed through these outbursts. Or they blamed the family for the child's problems. Mothers, in particular, were singled out as bad parents.

The idea that mental illness caused TS, and those who had TS could somehow control their actions, persisted until the 1960s. Since that time, doctors have come to realize what Gilles de la Tourette knew from the start: *Tourette syndrome is a physical illness, and people who have it cannot control what they do and say.* Yet old, false thinking lingers, even among some in the medical community. That's why it is so important to share the facts about this unusual condition.

IS TOURETTE SYNDROME CATCHING?

A common question for someone with Tourette syndrome is, "How did you get it?" Sometimes, the question comes from a deeper concern that TS is contagious, or catching, like the flu. The answer is *definitely not*! Although the exact cause of TS remains unclear, scientists do know it is never contagious.

People with TS are born with a tendency toward the condition, much as they are born with a specific color hair or eyes. This tendency may come from several different sources.

Brain Messages

Recent research shows that TS is a breakdown in how different parts of the brain send messages. The likely seat of the problem lies in the *basal ganglia*. These nerve cell clusters deep within the brain play a vital role in smooth muscle actions and stopping and starting movements (Fig. 3.1).

Researchers base their claim on the fact that the basal ganglia are involved in other movement disorders, such as Parkinson's disease and Huntington's chorea. With these diseases, uncontrolled movements result from nerve cell decay. As the cells weaken, the brain produces less of the neurotransmitter *dopamine*. *Neurotransmitters* are brain chemicals that carry signals from one nerve cell to another. Without this communication, nerve pathways become tense, causing rigid muscles and shaky, slow movements.

Unlike Parkinson's, nerve cells in TS seem to produce too much dopamine, making them extra sensitive to the chemical. One National Institute of Mental Health study identifies an area of the basal ganglia called the *caudate nucleus* as the source of the problem. The study compares brain scans of five pairs of identical twins who had TS. Findings show that the twin with more severe symptoms of TS displayed greater sensitivity in the caudate nucleus.[2] Excess dopamine covers the caudate nucleus, which reduces its ability to send messages from the brain to body parts that control movements.

Dopamine overloads trigger sudden spurts of uncontrolled movements. They cause failure of the

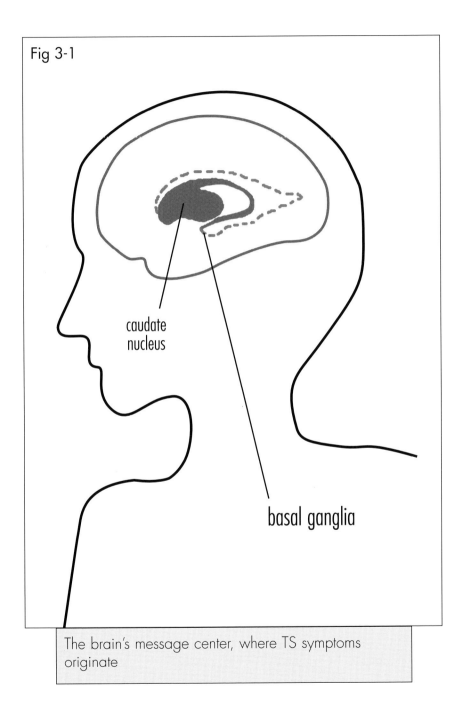

Fig 3-1

caudate
nucleus

basal ganglia

The brain's message center, where TS symptoms originate

normal brake system that controls unwanted impulses to move or speak. As a result, an impulse slips past the brakes, leading to a body jerk or unexpected sound. Tics are the brain's way of resolving chemical imbalances that may cause these uncontrolled movements. Several individuals with TS agree that tics are their brain's way of letting off steam to achieve balance. A similar response may develop from too little of the neurotransmitters *serotonin* and *norephinephrine*. Not enough of these chemicals can limit movement, which may also lead to tics.

Some scientists question whether slight differences in the brain's structure account for how nerve cells absorb chemicals. So far, studies point to differences in the size of the basal ganglia between patients with and without TS. One twin study reveals that the more affected twin has a 7 percent smaller right caudate nucleus. More research is in progress.

Infection

Scientists are also studying whether infection triggers TS. Normally, when infection invades the body, such as the disease-causing bacteria known as *strep*, the body creates substances called *antibodies* to fight off disease. The body uses antibodies to render germs from the infection harmless. Sometimes these antibodies get confused, and they attack healthy tissue in addition to the infection. In other words, the body attacks itself, which is called an *autoimmune reaction*.

Researchers believe that a small number of TS cases result from antibodies fighting strep infections that also attack nervous system tissue. Damage from antibodies causes changes in the basal ganglia. Each time someone prone to tics contracts strep or similar infections, symptoms flare, change, or worsen. Researchers further suggest that strep antibodies account for abnormal behavior and movements in obsessive-compulsive disorder, hyperactivity, and other tic disorders. The connection between strep infection and TS is still unclear but under study, too.

It's in the Genes

Various studies reveal that TS runs in families. *Genes* pass the trait for TS, and the brain's ability to regulate neurotransmitters, from parent to child. Genes are the tiniest bits of information that create traits in the body. Babies receive a set of genes from each parent when they are first conceived. If a child receives the same trait from each parent, the child has a greater likelihood of having that characteristic, whether it be blond hair or TS. If only one parent passes on the gene for a given trait, the child has much less chance of acquiring the characteristic. With TS, a parent of either sex can transmit the disorder.

Researchers believe humans have about 30,000 genes. Together, these genes provide the blueprint that makes each individual unique. Genes contain all the biological information needed for a person to develop before and after birth. But a problem with one or more gene can severely affect an individual's life.

The Human Genome (gene) Project, a federally funded study, hopes to map out where the gene for each trait lies, which is a massive project. So far, researchers know where on the map to look for the source of TS. But they haven't discovered the exact site yet. They just know it is caused in part by one or more abnormal genes.

One striking study that indicates TS is inherited involves triplets who were born in Sweden during the 1930s. Different families adopted each baby shortly after birth. The two girls and one boy each developed TS at age five, suggesting that Tourette syndrome passes from one generation to another. Forty-seven years later, the sisters and brother reunited. Interestingly, the triplets developed different tic behaviors. The man's only symptom was frequent blinking. One sister blinked and produced facial tics that traveled down her body and turned into leg kicking. The other sister displayed more severe signs: head and shoulder jerks, leg movements, facial tics, and grunts. [3]

Twin and triplet studies offer valuable understanding of how genes and environment influence disease. The Swedish study shows the powerful role genes play in TS. But it also points to the environment as a key factor in altering the type and frequency of tics.

Theories abound about events occurring before and after a baby is born that may change how the brain develops. Did the brain receive too little oxygen before or during birth? Did the baby receive too few nutrients before or after birth, which would keep weight down and slow brain growth? More recent twin studies point to brain size and birth weight as predictors of more severe tics in later life. Here, too, further research is needed.

HOW OFTEN DOES TS OCCUR?

The good news from the Human Genome Project indicates that TS is most likely a multigene disorder. If a single gene were responsible, only one gene from either parent would be enough to cause an offspring to tic. But researchers believe that TS comes from a combination of genes. Therefore, one or both parents must contribute the right combination of genes for TS or related disorders for their child to reveal signs of TS.

Above, identical twins Jared, left, and Joel, right.
Below, each experiences a motor tic.

For example, if a parent has TS, the likelihood of a child acquiring any form of tic disorder is about 50 percent for boys and 30 percent for girls. The odds of having TS serious enough to seek medical attention are much less, only about 10 percent. Even if a child gets TS, chances are symptoms will be mild or nonexistent. They may vary in the type, strength, and frequency of tics. Or they may show up as obsessive-compulsive behaviors or attention and learning problems without any tics. There is also the possibility that a gene-carrying child will never develop TS symptoms. What studies show for sure is that families with Tourette syndrome have a higher than normal risk of mild tic disorders and obsessive-compulsive behaviors than those in the general population.

PEOPLE WITH TOURETTE SYNDROME

Tourette syndrome is more common than once believed. Recent studies estimate that TS affects about one in 2,500 people in the United States. For some reason, the number climbs to one in 1,000 for boys. Almost four times as many boys have TS than girls. In fact, boys are three to five times more likely than girls to have most disorders related to learning, speech, and behavior. Not all boys with TS genes will develop a serious case. But almost all will experience some tic-related behaviors during their lifetime. By comparison, girls with the gene have only a 56 to 70 percent chance of developing tics.

Scientists differ about why this is so. Some think more boys may get diagnosed because they tend to act out more, which cannot be ignored, while girls display more nervous habits and repeat actions. Other researchers consider the physical differences between genders. Sex-related hormones, such as the male-oriented *testosterone*, may play a role in what TS symptoms boys and girls acquire. The sharp rise in hormones during adolescence could be a reason why tics seem to worsen during puberty and fade a few years later. In fact, about 20 to 30 percent of TS cases disappear completely by adulthood.

Besides their tics, people who live with TS are just like anyone else. They display the same range of intellect, interests, and feelings as people without Tourettes, and they live a normal life span.

As Jake says: "You are perfectly normal if you have TS. I bet you I could name something wrong with every person in our entire school. We just have tics. We cannot help it. We're not any better than you, and we're not any worse off. We should never be treated differently, except maybe for the tics."

FUTURE RESEARCH

Modern research brings up a wealth of important issues. If identical twins both tend toward having TS, why does one exhibit more severe symptoms than the other? What role does environment, including pollution, infection, or stress, play in determining the severity of these behaviors?

Then there is the whole area of prevention. What if scientists succeed in identifying abnormal brain patterns or genes that result in TS symptoms? Could they then eliminate TS by screening babies *before* they are born and treating the condition? Or could they protect children from ever being exposed to TS triggers in the environment? The challenge for the future will be to discover answers to these questions.

Chapter Four

WHAT TREATMENTS REDUCE TICS?

Most cases of Tourette syndrome require no treatment. Tics are so mild that they never interfere with everyday activities. Should they worsen, moderate symptoms can usually be controlled by reducing stress, making minor lifestyle changes, and educating others about TS. A small number of people, however, find their tics so troublesome that they seek treatment. For these individuals, the greatest difficulty lies in the fact that Tourette syndrome has no cure. But remedies *are* available to reduce the effects of TS on daily life.

MEDICATION

"If a child's tics don't get in the way, let him tic," Jake's mother suggests. "You don't want him medicated unless you have no choice."

The most effective way to calm tics is with medication. Many different drugs counter the chemical imbalance that results in tics. Not all common TS medications

work for everyone, though, and some may reduce one tic but not another. Patients often try several medications before finding the correct combination of one or more medicines and doses. Even then, unwanted side effects can blunt the benefits of fewer tics. Equally annoying, some medicines lose their punch after a while. Constant monitoring between families and physicians who know about TS is important to help kids feel their best.

Doctors most likely to be familiar with TS medications are *pediatricians,* who treat children and adolescents, *neurologists* who concentrate on the nervous system, and *psychiatrists,* who manage behavior and can prescribe medication. These specialists usually begin treatment by ordering low doses of medication. They suggest taking each new medicine for at least a couple of weeks, until it reaches the right level in the blood to work. If needed, changes in doses or types of medicine are given gradually and one at a time. That way, the patient, parents, and teachers can observe reactions to the medication—good or bad. Some doctors recommend keeping a diary to record results of different medicines. Complete records help patients, together with their physicians, decide whether or not a medication is for them.

Anti-tic Medicines

A common class of medications prescribed for TS is *neuroleptics.* These medicines suppress action of the brain chemical dopamine, which can decrease motor and vocal tics. Two frequently recommended neuroleptics are Haldol (the brand name for haloperidol) and Orap (the brand name for pimozide).

For a long time, Haldol has been the main neuroleptic doctors have tried, and some patients rely on it to ease their tics. But neuroleptics often cause side effects that are more troublesome than tics. Some people complain of sleepiness, restlessness, or slow thinking. Others struggle with weight gain, memory loss, stiff muscles, dry mouth, blurred vision, constipation, or depression. Orap and other neuroleptics may produce similar side effects but only when given at higher doses. Even with these problems, many people choose to stay on medicine rather than tic.

"I was on Haldol for almost three years," Mark recalls. "My side effects were getting sleepy and a huge weight gain. In high school I weighed over 220 pounds. I couldn't stay awake, my mouth was dry, and I was always eating. The side effects were almost as bad as the TS, so I tried a bunch of other medications. I went through about seven medications in two years, and nothing worked except Haldol. I continued on Haldol until the end of my freshman year at college."

In rare cases, treatment with neuroleptics produces *tardive dyskinesia*. This movement disorder involves random muscle actions, similar to TS. With tardive dyskinesia, most movements appear around the mouth, but they may spread throughout the body as slow, snakelike arm and leg motions and quick eyelid twitches. Tardive dyskinesia results from long-term use of neuroleptics. Symptoms usually but not always disappear when medicine leaves the body.

Another popular anti-tic medication is Catapres (clonidine), a drug for high blood pressure. Catapres seems to produce fewer side effects and long-term problems than neuroleptics. Sleepiness and dry mouth, the main difficulties, lessen with time. But so does the drug's ability to work.

A recent study indicates that *nicotine* eases symptoms of Tourette syndrome. Nicotine is the drug in tobacco that makes smoking addictive. It also increases manufacture of the chemical dopamine. Usually, TS symptoms come from too much dopamine. But nicotine floods the dopamine receptors enough so they shut down completely. No doctors recommend that anyone—especially children—smoke, because smoking causes a host of other problems. Rather, some doctors suggest that those patients with the most severe tics try nicotine gum or patches. A patch is worn directly on the skin and delivers a small, even dose of nicotine to lesson the cravings associated with nicotine with-drawal. Thus, someone wearing a patch gets a small, even dose of nicotine.

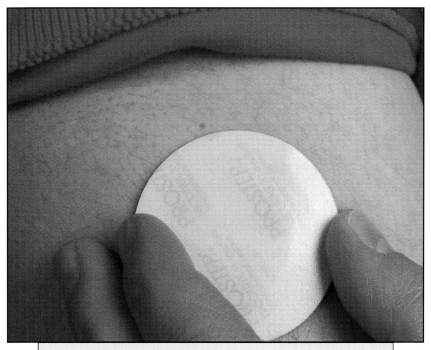

A nicotine patch. Releasing low levels of nicotine into the body has been shown to reduce tics for some people with TS.

Nicotine treatment for TS symptoms is not for everyone. Seventy percent of children who have tried the patch complain of skin irritation and nausea. Research is under way to study drugs that act the same way as nicotine in the brain but will not produce unwanted side effects. One such drug is *mecamylamine*, another blood pressure drug.

As doctors learn more about specific chemicals involved in TS, they experiment with a host of other medications that may serve different patients better. Information about newer medications and their effects is available from the Tourette Syndrome Association and Web sites mentioned in the Resources section of this book.

Medications for Conditions Related to TS

For some children, tics are the least of their problems. Poor attention, mind-numbing obsessions, panic attacks, or mood swings spell more trouble than classic TS symptoms. These other conditions often require greater attention. Yet medication effects on the range of symptoms that may accompany TS vary. Drugs that work best with ADD may increase tics. Others that control tics may increase depression or obsessions. Treatment becomes a dance to calm the most serious behavior without arousing the others.

"We find that symptoms keep evolving," Adam's mother explains. "We always look at what is most serious. Is his inability to focus in class the more serious problem? Or is he about to be kicked out of school for behavior problems? Is he picking mosquito bites so ferociously that he drips blood? We constantly weigh what is worse and have him on a variety of medications based on that evaluation."

In the few cases where symptoms are linked to strep infection, the choice of medication is easy: antibiotics.

For most cases, however, the choice of medication is more complicated. Two main types of medications that balance TS-related symptoms are *stimulants* and *tranquilizers*. Each produces a change in one or more brain chemicals that affect behavior.

Stimulants boost the flow of norephinephrine and dopamine. For some reason, this calms children with ADD/ADHD, allowing them to pay attention longer in school. As with TS medication, however, stimulants can have unpleasant side effects. The popular drug Ritalin (methylphenidate) often causes nervousness or impairs sleeping and eating. When either occurs, doctors may play with the timing of doses. For example, some suggest taking medication only on school days, when paying attention in class is important.

More serious problems can occur because stimulants may stunt body growth or trigger or increase tics. Taking regular vacations from the drug helps prevent slowed growth. If mounting tics become a problem, doctors usually recommend switching to a tranquilizer, or antidepressant. These medications smooth the action of neurotransmitters. Sometimes, tranquilizers have the added benefit of reducing uncontrollable obsessions, compulsions, and depression. But they can cause blurred vision, dry mouth, muscle twitches, and constipation. Some children become so sleepy they are unable to get out of bed in the morning, let alone learn.

"I was given a lot of prescription drugs that gave me bad side effects," Brian agrees. "One medication caused me to be unable to urinate [which is rare], even in the morning when you really have to go. Suddenly you have no control over something you take for granted. It makes a bad situation worse. You have one problem that people stare at you about, and then you have reactions from medication. Now I take two different medications, one for anxiety attacks and one for depression. These have done wonders. Both are tranquilizers that give me an overall feeling of calm, which helps with TS."

Sometimes, doctors prescribe a combination of drugs to balance different TS symptoms. With any of these medications, close observation is important to prevent interactions. Mixing chemicals of any kind—for example, by taking medication and drinking alcohol, or smoking or sniffing drugs—can cause serious trouble. Therefore, someone taking powerful medications needs to check with the doctor before taking even the mildest over-the-counter cold medication.

"The doctor prescribed a cough medicine when my son got sick," Raymond's mother remembers. "He shouldn't have had that medication. His blood pressure was so high he was flying, and we didn't know. He went to the school nurse because he was acting funny. She took his blood pressure and said this kid is off the wall. By then, we realized it was the mix of drugs the doctor prescribed. We switched doctors after that."

TREATMENT WITHOUT MEDICATION

Diet

Doctors differ about how much diet affects TS behavior. A few physicians favor strict diets that limit certain types of foods, while others suggest that food has nothing to do with how someone behaves. Yet many parents report changes in their child after several weeks of limiting specific foods. Common problem foods are sugary snacks, junk foods (chips, white bread, fried treats), dairy products, caffeine drinks, chocolate, and tomatoes. Most often, parents notice a decrease in their hyper child's activity level.

In some cases, a food allergy causes changes in behavior. There are two ways to test for food allergies.

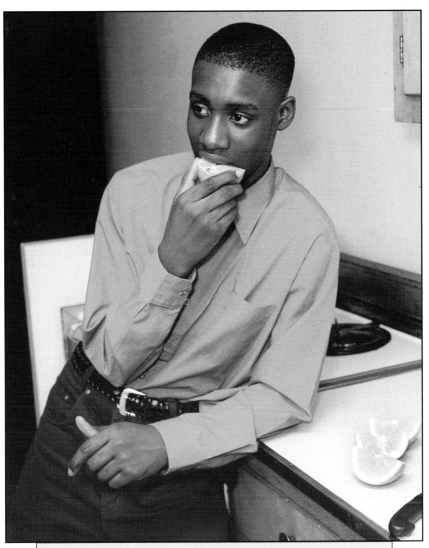

Making better food choices, such as eliminating junk food and snacking on fruit instead, improves the quality of a person's diet. Some doctors believe this leads to better balance in the body's neurological system.

One is to eat a limited diet for a couple of weeks. Then add one food at a time, watching for behavior changes. Another method is to avoid eating food that is suspected to cause problems for two weeks. Add the questionable food and see if symptoms increase. If they do, eliminate that food from the diet. Otherwise, eat what is generally healthy for the body without adding food obsessions to the problem mix.

Vitamins and Food Supplements

Usually, the body manufactures the balance of vitamins it needs to run smoothly. Some researchers believe that when the body spins out of whack, as with TS, extra vitamins help restore balance and reduce signs of disorder. As with diet, specialists differ about the effectiveness of taking vitamins or any food supplements.

Supporters of vitamin therapy seem to believe more is better. Many critics question taking the large doses needed to make a difference. In addition, vitamins and supplements require no prescription and are not government regulated. Therefore, studies about their effects and interactions with other drugs are limited. High doses of over-the-counter supplements that can be obtained without a doctor's supervision can cause serious disease that may go unnoticed.

One of the more common diet additions for TS-related disorders is vitamin B6. Vitamin B6 helps many chemicals in the brain work. Although some families report success with vitamin B6 and other nutrients, including blue-green algae, no formal studies verify these results. More research is needed in this area.

"We've tried nutritional supplements," Caroline's mother recalls. "We had a list about a mile long. Caroline also tried a special diet for a while. It's so hard to tell if anything worked. We thought these things

Vigorous, habitual hand washing, and other compulsive rituals, is a common manifestation of TS and its closely related "cousin," obsessive-compulsive disorder.

might be helping for a while, but she was also taking medication. We think it was more the medication than the supplements."

Surgery

Physicians in Europe have experimented with surgery to reduce severe ticcing. The surgery involves implanting electrodes in the brain. Then electrical charges are sent into the basal ganglia, site of the excess activity that causes tics. By charging different parts of the basal ganglia, doctors are able to reduce motor and vocal tics. Over time, the charges are repeated until tics fade. Although appealing as a quick fix, this treatment has not been tried enough to evaluate. Surgery can be hazardous, and the treatment is considered experimental and only for extreme cases.

Cognitive Therapy

Many children who have TS with obsessions benefit from *cognitive therapy*. With this treatment, a trained therapist presents an orderly way to track unwanted behaviors, such as excessive hand washing or asking too many questions in class. The patient records each time hand washing occurs, noting particular situations that trigger the scrubbing. Then the therapist sees how close to the triggers someone can get without feeling the need to wash the hands. The therapist suggests more acceptable behaviors for these times, retraining the brain to react differently to specific situations.

"Cognitive therapy helped me become more aware of my tics," Raymond believes. Now he is aware of when he needs to raise his hand in class and how much anxiety he can stand before he is forced to do it. When the urge to ask a question arises, Raymond sits on his hand. He learned to raise his hand every other time instead of every time. He still works on improving.

Biofeedback

People tone their body through exercise. Some therapists claim that children and adults tone the brain
through *biofeedback*. This training program enhances
awareness of the body's automatic and unconscious
processes, such as tics and restlessness, so they can be
controlled. With biofeedback, the patient sits at a computer or other monitoring device. Small sensors run
from the scalp to the computer. The machine relays
information about the body's responses back to the

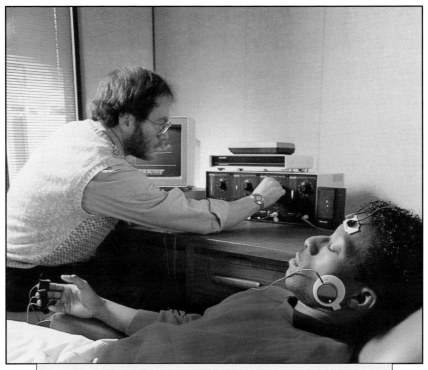

A series of biofeedback sessions can help a person
recognize physical responses to stress and, for some
with TS, assist in identifying tic triggers.

individual as sounds, numbers, or pictures. Gradually, patients learn to connect these cues with how they feel when body functions change.

Biofeedback is a common tool for treating stress-related conditions. Some therapists credit brain exercises with improving attention and general behavior. Others counter that anybody would improve with the amount of time and attention biofeedback requires. And the cost is high. A full course of treatment includes twenty to forty hours for between $1,500 and $5,000. Another problem is the willingness of someone to sit still and concentrate.

"I think biofeedback caused more stress than it alleviated," Caroline's mother remembers. "You have to be cooperative to get anywhere, and Caroline didn't care about it."

Chapter Five

HOME AND SCHOOL

When Jake was five, he bashed his action figures together to cover clicking noises from his mouth—sounds beyond his control. By second grade, his shoulders shrugged and his hands flicked uncontrollably in addition to the sounds. At night, his body twitched and jerked for hours before allowing him to fall asleep. Without enough sleep, Jake had trouble getting up for school and often felt drowsy in class. Staying awake grew even more difficult after he was diagnosed with Tourette syndrome and treated with medication that caused drowsiness as a side effect.

As years went by, the involuntary movements changed. Jake's head jerked. His sounds boomed louder. With these body changes, Jake became less able to sit still and concentrate. For years he had liked school and earned good grades. By fifth grade, however, he found it harder to focus on his work and what the teacher said.

By junior high, Jake hated school. He rarely picked up social clues from other people about how to act or react. He viewed anyone trying to help him or tell him what to do as a threat. He said teachers annoyed him. He picked fights. Quick to anger, he beat up kids who crossed him or mentioned his tics.

At home, Jake argued with his parents and seldom finished his schoolwork. He carefully lined up clothes in his room, even organized his sister's closet. But he couldn't remember to pack the right papers and books needed for homework. If he completed the work, he usually forgot it at home. Rather than ask for help, Jake either blew up or shut down completely. His life became a constant struggle.

AT HOME

The effects of Tourette syndrome extend beyond the person in the family who has it. The condition alters relationships with parents, brothers and sisters, teachers, and classmates.

Parents

Parents naturally want the best for their children. They often dream about their offspring's bright future. None of these visions includes tics. Hearing a diagnosis of TS unleashes a jumble of emotions. Many parents who have been searching for answers feel relieved to discover their child has something medically wrong. For them, the process of finding help can begin. But other parents feel guilty for possibly passing TS on to their child and angry at the unfair blow to their family. They may think they are bad parents, especially when others judge them as either overprotective or unable to control their child.

Parents who work hard and value education wonder how their child could seem so lax about school. They cannot understand that their child is not careless or lazy but unable to focus because of TS and its silent relatives. With coaxing their child to work harder, visiting doctors frequently, and explaining TS to themselves and others, most parents are simply exhausted.

"People make judgments about the child and parenting based solely on what they see," Aaron's mother admits. "They think that TS is just a tic, noises, or swear words. But it is so many things and so invasive. It's vague and hard to explain. You don't have the same kind of understanding and support as when you have a child in a wheelchair. With TS, your child has kind of an invisible disability."

Yet parents are key to helping someone with TS progress. They create the climate of support at home. They engineer ways to reduce their child's stress, which lessens tics. For example, they choose to take their child to movie theaters at times when few viewers attend. Or they plan escape routes to bathrooms or outdoors when tics disturb others in public places.

"We came to realize that certain situations don't work for us," Aaron's mother adds. "So we don't put ourselves in them. With Aaron, behavior issues from his ADHD make sitting still in a restaurant difficult for him. We've also learned not to put him in other situations, such as bringing him to a long show, or to temple or church, or out to dinner with friends. We accept limitations and say this doesn't work for us."

Often, the parents' main job involves listening to their child, trying to figure out what actions and words really mean. For example, one mother wanted to stop her son from raging when she refused to take him shopping. Instead of saying "yes" or "no," she listened to the request and parroted what she heard back to her son. That way, he knew she understood correctly. As her son talked more, he revealed that his real problem was getting stuck, or obsessing, on going to buy an item. He felt worse about having this obsession than about not being allowed to go to the store. Once he felt understood, his tension subsided and the rages calmed.

When children feel supported and accepted, they learn to deal with TS better. They realize that home is a safe place to tic and relieve tension. Moreover, children who have supportive parents learn that they are much more than just their tics. They are individuals with many skills that will flower as they age.

"As a parent, you cannot imagine having to cope with certain kinds of things, but you find you can cope with anything," Aaron's mother explains. "You also want to model and set good examples for your children. If you can't cope with what he has, how can he? You have to tell your child he or she is a fantastic person. And yes, you have a lot of things to cope with. But you are coping with them, and I am glad you are."

Sisters and Brothers

When one sibling has TS, it distorts the normal relationship between sisters and brothers. Siblings commonly bicker and compete for attention and individual recognition. But such rivalry takes on new meaning when the sibling with TS plays by different rules, ones they cannot control.

Siblings without TS understandably become angry with a brother who randomly punches them or grunts during TV shows. They are frustrated with a sister who plows through game boards or breaks toys. They may resent the extra attention TS requires and hate the worry and uproar their sibling causes the family. Before a diagnosis is made, they may punch back at siblings who touch or yell at them to stop making noises. Once the diagnosis is confirmed, they may feel guilty for disliking someone with a problem.

Sibling reactions differ with age and the extent TS disrupts family routines. For younger children, jealousy is a common reaction to feeling left out or neglected. They may imitate their sibling with TS to get attention or worry they somehow caused the tics. Sometimes, siblings believe that because they do not have TS, their problems are not worth mentioning. Instead, they either try to be perfect or cause trouble, anything to get their parent's attention. Each approach usually leads to resentment or trouble. If parents overprotect the child with TS, siblings may resent being blamed for whatever happens between the two or being held to a higher standard. If parents never explain TS to them, siblings worry that something more serious has happened to their sister or brother.

"I thought my brother was going to die," a 24-year-old sibling remembered. "My parents whispered about his condition behind closed doors. Nobody told me anything. I could have been more supportive when we were in junior high and high school if I'd only known what was going on. I thought he was doing them [tics] on purpose." [1]

As children mature, they feel embarrassed about living with someone who acts so weird. Preteens and teens, in particular, try to fit in, rarely wanting to call attention to themselves. Being with someone who tics wildly or makes noises is like wearing a neon sign that screams, "Look at me." So older sisters and brothers often refuse to be seen with their sibling or to go on family outings. They never invite friends home, fearing outsiders would learn of their less-than-average family.

Brothers and sisters of any age worry that TS is catching. And many live in fear of a sibling who rages.

"I could wake up in a bad mood," Brian recalls. "I would say to my brother, 'I don't like what you are watching on TV.' I gave him a lot of verbal abuse for the littlest things. For the most part it was me yelling, making a fool of myself. There were times I was so out of control, however, that I saw horror in his eyes. He cried sometimes. It doesn't make me feel good that my own brother was afraid of me. I can't believe how awful it was for him."

Parents play the biggest role in helping siblings get along. If parents practice patience and understanding, so will sisters and brothers. Part of understanding comes with learning about TS. Information why a sibling behaves a certain way reduces fears and resentment. In addition, facts arm siblings with answers to questions from friends and classmates, who may tease or belittle them for living with TS. Many siblings find booklets and videos from the Tourette Syndrome Association helpful to learn about TS themselves and to share with others.

Another important factor in family harmony is communication. One way to open communication is to hold regular family meetings. Weekly meetings give all members of the family a place to air their feelings and concerns. They provide a time when everyone listens without judgment. Then the family can discuss solutions to problems together. Individuals involved in a problem can role-play, perhaps taking each other's part. Seeing how someone else looks acting like another family member often triggers humor, which reduces tension.

As one younger sibling of a brother with TS notes, "It's important to get each person's perspective—both

Making time for regular, informal chats in the comfort of the family kitchen is a rewarding way for families to keep a balanced perspective on dealing with TS and other issues.

sides of the story. Talking things out makes living together better." [2]

Besides meetings, parents need to make regular time for each child, not just the one with TS. Having special time with parents lets children know they are special. During these times, parents can reassure each child of their love and resolve to keep them and their belongings safe. Parents can help siblings understand that TS behaviors are the problem, not their sister or brother. Perhaps parents can talk about *their* frustrations with TS and what *they* do to feel better. For example, some parents leave the room or punch a pillow when anger arises. Once siblings feel heard and understood, many resent their sibling with TS less and begin to value them for being who they are.

"Peter Hollenbeck, a professor at Purdue University, states that his older brothers . . . made fun of everything but [his] tics. Being treated like any other little brother gave (him) the self-confidence he needed to face people who were not always so accepting." [3]

GETTING HELP OUTSIDE THE HOME

Support Groups

People often wonder how someone with TS could escape diagnosis for so long. For many who tic, the answer is clear. They were born that way. Tics are part of them, so they never knew to feel any other way or that how they acted had a specific name. Since most people with TS see extremes portrayed in the media or books, they never connected themselves with those images.

Once people who tic get together, as in support groups or association meetings, something strange happens. They find an instant bond. They share similar experiences. They see others who struggle with tics and still succeed—in school, with friends, on the job. Joining a support group helps to balance feelings of isolation and feeling different. Someone with TS is no longer alone.

The same holds for parent and sibling support groups. Only someone who has walked in their shoes can understand the frustrations of living with someone who has TS. Parents compare medications and techniques for handling behaviors. They deal with feelings of guilt and sorrow at not being able to prevent or cure their child's tics. Siblings learn ways to deal with the

A support group "rap session" provides a safe place for people dealing with TS to discharge difficult emotions and gain a sense of being heard and understood.

embarrassment of living with someone who acts oddly. They discover inner strengths for handling a brother or sister who swears or throws things. TS groups reduce the isolation from non-TS families who seem more normal. Families can find various support groups through their local Tourette Syndrome Association or doctor.

"I thought I was the only one who had a kid that has TS," Jake's mother remembers. "I wondered what I did to my kid? I met this woman at the group who said this is a normal reaction from parents. I felt relieved."

Professional Therapy

When Tourette syndrome makes families spin out of control, they need to seek professional help. Individual therapy with a licensed psychologist, psychiatrist, or social worker who has had experience with TS can help family members sort out their feelings. The person with TS learns methods of getting along better with others that enhance medication therapy.

Family therapy, where everyone is involved at the same time, puts the entire family on the same track. A therapist pinpoints when family members get stuck in routines that interfere with helpful communications. All members learn to work toward common goals as all assume responsibility for how they behave.

TS GOES TO SCHOOL

Children with mild tics find that their TS rarely interferes with schoolwork. But school can be a nightmare for those with frequent tics or other related problems. Consider the embarrassment; the inability to control the body long enough to sit still and stay quiet; medication that causes sleepiness, nausea, and dizziness; the lack of problem solving, organizing, and social skills. Add possible learning disabilities, obsessions, compulsions, mood swings, and rage attacks, and school can feel more like a battleground than a place to learn.

Schoolwork Blues

Take reading, for example. How many people could read a long paragraph while their head jerks? Could they understand the paragraph if they *had* to count the number of a's in each sentence? How could they finish in the allotted time when their need to read each letter in order forces them to start over repeatedly?

What about writing with hand and arm tics or blinking eyes? And then there is math. Some people with TS have an obsession about a certain number. They fear that writing or reading the number will cause something awful to happen. Who could complete a test while following rituals to avoid this number? How can they convince a teacher they want to cooperate but are stuck with a notion in their head that refuses to go away?

"Paying attention was an effort for Joel," his mother says. "He would get off into some of his thoughts. He said his mind wandered. His handwriting was so bad his tests were illegible. Teachers would give work back. He had trouble taking notes, listening, and being able to take tests. It was overwhelming for him. Changing class was overwhelming, too. He was a mess going from one class to another nine times a day. He took many minutes to settle down. He was always losing books. He never wrote assignments in his calendar, partly from not wanting to and partly because it was difficult to organize."

Explaining Tourette Syndrome

The law guarantees all children an education. How they receive that education may vary, depending on the severity of TS. Most children with TS can learn in regular classes. Some benefit from going to a *resource room* for part of the day. Here, a specially trained teacher works with fewer students at a time. Resource teachers adapt regular classroom assignments and help students organize what they learn. When needed, they support individuals in their regular classes.

If students require constant support, such as for extreme behavior problems, the school district may hire an aide to shadow them (follow and observe them from class to class). If students are still unable to handle a regular classroom, they may be referred to a *special needs class* or a special school in a different building. Such placements are done according to specific guidelines with input from teachers, parents, and the school psychologist. In rare cases, parents decide to teach their child themselves at home. The idea is to find the right setting to help each child learn better.

Usually, minor changes and extra aid are enough to help someone with tics or learning and attention problems succeed. The first step is educating school personnel about TS. Too many uninformed teachers believe that a child with TS tics on purpose. Because kids often hide or delay expressing their tics, adults assume they *can* be controlled.

Parents can do their part by alerting teachers that a child has TS. They should explain that TS is a neurological condition that cannot be controlled and suggest that teachers ignore tics and devise safeguards, such as those described in the next section, to reduce triggers. For their part, teachers need an extra dose of patience and creativity to work with TS students. The Tourette Syndrome Association and other associations listed in the Resources section of this book offer booklets for teachers that describe symptoms and suggest ways to manage TS and related symptoms in the classroom.

"Each year I revise a letter I keep in my computer that goes to Adam's teachers before school begins," his mother says. "I lay out what his strengths and symptoms are and update what kind of medication he takes and how it affects him. I also tell the teacher what has worked in the past and urge teachers to call me if there are any problems. Some parents prefer to be there and talk to the teacher the first day of school, and that works well. But for us the letter works."

Many parents worry that their child with TS will be teased by classmates. When their child agrees, parents may ask teachers to talk with classmates or offer to do it themselves. In some cases, learning about TS is enough to stop bullying. But merely having information does not automatically bring friends.

"When I was diagnosed, my teacher sat in front of the whole class and said 'Raymond has TS, and this is what it is,'" Ray remembers. "I think that helps me because it lets me know that if someone accepts it [TS], they are my friend. If they don't, they're not worth being friends with."

Building Success into Learning

Here are some classroom tips that may lessen the impact of TS symptoms on learning:

Seating. Teachers can help students with Tourettes by asking them where they want to sit. Students with frequent tics may prefer a desk in the back where others cannot see the movements or be as bothered by noises. Or they may choose to sit near the door, so they can leave if the urge to tic becomes overwhelming. If paying attention is a problem, they may benefit from sitting away from windows and doorways at a desk with a clear view of the teacher. Desks should be free of unnecessary materials and nearby walls cleared of anything distracting. Some students find they can work better with a portable screen or divider around their desk or in another room.

Special codes. Agreed-upon signals can help students with TS and their teachers communicate without interrupting classes. Teachers may say code words or use hand signals to remind the student to pay attention. Similarly, students can touch an ear or raise two fingers to signal the need to be excused when tics are over-powering and they feel a need to move around. A teacher and student can arrange a safe place where the student can go to tic.

Timing and tests. Constant tics take time and can be tiring. Short breaks during intense work periods reduce the strain of holding back the urge to tic. Untimed tests, which also reduce stress, make up for the extra time it takes to tic. Many students ask to take tests in a private room. Then they do not waste energy trying to suppress tics that disturb other students.

Transitions. Teachers can help students manage changes in routine by reminding them what is going to happen before the change takes place. Children who find transitions difficult work better with established routines. A written list of tasks for the day lets them check off each activity or project as it occurs. For example, the list can be in an assignment book that always stays with the student. Parents and teachers can work together to review directions and items needed to complete homework assignments. The more structure to the school day, the easier it is for a disorganized student to manage.

Adjusted assignments. Students with TS need some slack in completing their tasks and should not be punished for turning in homework late. Those who have added ADD require simple and easy-to-follow instructions. Tasks should be assigned one at a time and then completed before moving to the next task. Too much work assigned together can be overwhelming, so teachers need to reduce assignments and break them into smaller parts. For example, half a page of science questions or every other math problem on a page is easier to handle than an entire page. For major projects, the teacher or parent can work with the student to complete one step at a time until the entire job is done.

A student with attention difficulties focuses on her mid-term exams in an isolated corner of the school gym.

Students can learn to break assignments into smaller tasks themselves. One way is to cut or fold worksheets into sections to work on one problem in each. Markers are helpful to highlight or color-code important information or different subjects. When reading long sections, students can cut a rectangle the height and width of one line from a piece of cardboard that is the size of the book page. The cutout helps wandering eyes focus on words inside the opening while blocking out the rest of the page.

Taking notes can be a problem for students who cannot concentrate or write quickly. Some teachers assign a note-taking partner who can share copies of notes and assignments. For students unable to focus, other teachers prepare notes, highlighted copies of textbook pages, or samples of what they want, such as completed math problems or answered questions. To avoid homework hell at home, parents sometimes hire a homework buddy or professional tutor to keep the student up with the class.

Learning aids. Modern technology and a little inventiveness provide many aids for students in the classroom.

- Calculators reduce carelessness in solving math problems.
- Computers help students who write poorly.
- Headsets block out distracting sounds while at work.
- Tape recorders take notes when students cannot write quickly or focus. Many teachers allow students with unreadable handwriting to tape test answers. Books on tape enable students to listen and absorb a story faster than reading if they have head jerks, obsessions, or constantly blinking eyes. Some students can focus better when they listen to a tape that beeps at regular intervals, such as every minute. The beep jogs them out of a daydream or getting stuck on a thought.
- A foam rubber mat placed on top of the desk cushions sounds from annoying tapping tics.

- Graph paper or notebook paper turned sideways helps students write numbers for math problems in straight columns.
- Color-coded folders or separators for three-ring binders organize papers for different subjects.
- Two sets of textbooks, one to keep in class and one to keep at home, relieve the problem of remembering to bring the correct book home. Extra sets of school supplies at each location guard against forgetting.

Students need to learn how to be their own advocates at school. If something is not working for them, they need to ask parents and teachers for help. Although symptoms of TS may make school harder, it need not be impossible. A little creativity goes a long way toward making learning easier.

Chapter Six

LEARNING TO LIVE WITH TOURETTE SYNDROME

Picture someone walking calmly down the hall and suddenly breaking into a hop-skip, arms punching the air. People stare. Others quickly move away or yell names, like "psycho" or "weirdo." Now imagine another person watching a movie in a quiet theater. Suddenly, his or her loud grunts, curses, or racial slurs pierce the silence. Viewers within hearing distance yell at the person to be still. A few viewers raise their fists at insults that hurt their feelings.

How should people with these tics react, knowing they cannot prevent what their body does? Should they fight back? Should they refuse to go out in public? Or could they learn to live with the changing mix of uncontrollable behaviors that comes with Tourette syndrome?

These situations and more are what many people who have TS face every day. As one doctor says,

"Living with Tourette syndrome means constantly explaining that you're not crazy, that you're not doing it on purpose, that you just happen to have a neurological [nervous system] disorder."[1]

FEELING BETTER ABOUT YOURSELF

Self-esteem can take a beating when TS accompanies the normal pressures of growing up. Extra criticism, punishment, and teasing add to the embarrassment and frustration of TS-related symptoms. But having TS should not stop anyone from experiencing the world. Activities may take extra time and planning, and there will be disappointments along with the successes. But successes will happen. Once people accept their TS, they will feel more comfortable with themselves. Then they are ready to seek friends, play instruments, join sports teams, date, work, and drive—whatever kids their age do.

"In order to live with Tourette syndrome, I think we must learn to live—period," writes William Rubin, a psychologist and researcher who has TS. "That is, we must focus on things we would do if we did not have TS, and figure out ways to accomplish these things. . . . There is no way to totally ignore the many additional problems TS creates for us. But the more we can try to live our lives as others do, the better able we will be to handle the special burdens placed on us by the symptoms of TS."[2]

Building on Strengths

Anything that builds on interests, hobbies, and talents is more likely than not to bring success. And nothing develops positive self-esteem better than success. So why not arrange more activities that increase the likelihood that success will occur?

Solitary, non-competitive activities like jogging can help build stamina and enhance self-esteem.

For example, teens who like to write might join the school newspaper or yearbook staff, or they may keep a diary or journal. Those who love sports might sign up for a school or community team sport. If team sports pose problems, sports lovers might consider noncontact sports, such as jogging, swimming, or tai chi. Animal lovers might buy a pet, offer to dog-sit for a neighbor, or seek a job at the local pet store. Each small success raises self-esteem another notch.

Taking Control of Life

Gaining independence is another way to build self-esteem. Individuals who do things on their own feel better about themselves. Too often, however, families and schools use TS as an excuse. Parents and teachers never push the child with tics to excel, or the child refuses to try. People assume that TS prevents someone from performing, so they never ask the person to join activities. These people believe they are helping, but they are actually sending the message that someone with TS is less capable.

"My parents actually use TS as an excuse against me," Raymond explains. "They say, 'We understand you cannot do this because of your tics.' It would upset me because I actually could do it, and they didn't give me the chance. They think of everything in terms of TS, instead of thinking I might be able to accomplish things with more time."

Children with TS cannot predict how others may react to them, and they cannot force other kids to be their friends. But they can control which situations they are in and their own responses. This means *taking responsibility* for their actions. Responsibility involves speaking up to change situations at home, school, and on the job to adjust for TS-related symptoms.

"You have to take responsibility for your symptoms," Mark stresses. "In TS camp, I teach that if you have motor tics, you may knock over a glass of water. I know you couldn't help it, but you should clean it up. You shouldn't have been that close. Similarly, if you have loud vocal tics, you should not be in a quiet room at the library. That's not being courteous, again, even though you cannot help it."

To Tell or Not to Tell

Many TS-related feelings and symptoms are invisible. Other people cannot read minds to understand why someone who tics says or does certain things. Therefore, communication becomes key to making life with TS easier. Yet people who tic differ about whether or not to be open about having TS. Several agree that the decision boils down to comfort level—with themselves and with their condition—and age. The older people are, the more open they seem about explaining to new people about their TS.

"I'm learning to be more outgoing," Raymond says. "In the past, I was very, very shy. Now I tell everyone I meet that I have TS, if I know them for more than one visit. Occasionally, people don't like it and shy away from me. Only one time was it used against me."

"Tell them the truth," Jake suggests, now, though he admits that when he was younger, "I wouldn't tell anyone the truth. I'd just say leave me alone. It depends upon your personality if you tell people."

"Only this year did I start to tell people, my really good friends," Caroline adds. "I wouldn't talk about it in the past, just recently."

"I had trouble when it [tics] was explained to people," Brian recalls. "When I was younger, it brought questions that I really didn't know how to answer at the time. Now if I know somebody will be in my life a long time, I tell them about TS. But I don't need to tell acquaintances when it doesn't come up—not that I'm ashamed of it."

HOW OTHERS CAN HELP SOMEONE WHO TICS

For many people with TS, social situations worsen their tics. They sense that friends, classmates, and family are watching and listening for symptoms. They feel uncomfortable with bullies who cannot understand them and with strangers who look worried about catching Tourette syndrome. Most individuals with TS wonder why others cannot learn to accept and get past the tics. They want classmates and coworkers to know there is a real person beyond the movements and sounds. Several teens and young adults have suggested how to help everyone involved with TS feel more comfortable:

"Don't tell jokes about it," Caroline advises. "Just act as if I wasn't doing anything. Somebody once was mean. It felt like a punch in the stomach."

"Support me and not bring it up," Raymond recommends. "I like talking about it sometimes, but others should make sure they don't offend me by saying anything."

"If someone tells you they have TS, believe them. Don't mimic them," Mark urges. "Don't ask them to repeat their tics because if they weren't ticcing, asking will set them off. Don't accuse them of being able to control tics. Don't try to be funny and respond to their coprolalia with a joke. Just try to be understanding that they cannot help it."

HELPING YOURSELF

Substituting One Action for Another

Some people find they can replace tics with more socially acceptable movements and still satisfy the original urge. They perform a movement similar to the orig-

85

inal tic. Substitutions help relieve tics that cause pain or danger, such as lip biting, head jerking, or wrist banging.

"I had this big sore in my mouth from biting," Caroline remembers. "I would scrape under it to relieve the urge, so it wouldn't hurt so much and it wouldn't be so noticeable."

"I mask putting my finger up my nose by blowing my nose," Mark explains. "And I try to cover up a grunt with a cough. I can also focus on somebody or something really intensely so I won't tic. I just have to find something to talk about and get going."

Learning to Relax

Studies show that when someone with Tourettes relaxes, so do their tics. But relaxing is easier said than done. Nowadays most children and adults with and without TS lead very scheduled, stress-filled lives. Therefore, it's important to carve out time to kick back and renew energy, which contributes to positive mental health.

Meditation. Some people believe meditation helps them tic less. This method of relaxing requires focusing on a single word or object, rather than music. Once the mind refocuses, it draws attention away from distracting thoughts that may cause stress. As stress leaves the mind, blood pressure goes down and muscle tension eases.

Exercise. Exercise is the best natural tranquilizer. Any form of exercise will do: walking, running, biking, swimming, dancing, playing sports. The main idea is to enjoy the activity enough to continue on a regular basis. Regular physical activity sparks production of brain chemicals that relieve depression and pent-up tension caused by the urge to tic. Another benefit of exercise is

Meditation is a mental discipline that addresses an array of problems a person with TS may face.

that it burns more calories as the body works faster. This helps control weight gain from medication. Afterward, exercise leaves the body at peace. For many people with TS, exercise reduces the frequency and force of their tics and eases the pain from muscles tightened due to repeated movements. Exercise also lessens symptoms of ADHD and OCD. Exercisers feel better all around in body and mind.

"I played soccer for the first three years of high school, and now I'm on the cross-country and track teams," Raymond agrees. "When I'm doing a sport, I tic a lot less because I'm not paying attention to everything. I'm thinking about the sport, like kicking the ball in soccer."

Relaxing to music. For individuals who have trouble staying still, music gives them purpose. Peaceful sounds, such as ocean waves or harp music, focus the brain. When the brain is occupied, the body becomes calmer. Studies confirm that music slows breathing and blood flow and lowers muscle tension, which may reduce tics and help the body rest.

Visualization. Research supports a strong connection between body and mind. Many people find that closing their eyes and creating a mental picture of health frees them of stress. They imagine the picture as detailed and real as possible. For example, people with wild arm and leg tics may envision their body lying still, with just one body part at a time gently moving. The idea behind visualization is for the mind to send the body a message that it is strong and can heal itself.

Yoga and tai chi. Two forms of exercise, yoga and tai chi, emphasize the mind/body connection. The ancient Hindu system of yoga combines deep breathing with physical poses that slowly stretch muscles through a series of exercises. Over time, yoga exercises can pro-

Like meditation, yoga integrates the mind with the body, increases relaxation, and produces a sense of well-being.

duce greater muscle strength and flexibility. The Chinese system of tai chi uses exercise and movement to increase body awareness and control. Each of the more than one hundred exercises begins with the body in a different position. Constant slow movements result in inner stillness. Tai chi fans believe that the exercises create a perfect union of body and mind. Although neither approach has been proven to affect tics, both are known to improve body tone and overall health and well-being.

FIGHTING DISCRIMINATION

Several laws protect the rights of people with disabilities. The laws guarantee access to education, jobs, public places, transportation, and government services. Even with these laws, discrimination happens. Kids with TS get suspended from school for being hyper, raging, or coprolalia. Adults who tic have difficulty finding and keeping jobs.

Several lawsuits have been filed against various organizations, such as airlines or housing developments, for refusing people with TS. In one case, a man was denied a job after successfully completing the company's training program. The results of his lawsuit, with the company paying him a large sum, resounded around the world after his lawyer's news conference.

"That [the conference] pleased me more than the money," the man said. "A lot of people learned about Tourette syndrome. I've never had any trouble working because of my condition; I didn't consider it a legal handicap. I knew what I could do. People with [TS] need to stand up for themselves." [3]

Individuals with TS who feel their rights have been trampled can contact the Tourette Syndrome Association, their local government department of disabilities or fair employment, or the Family Resource Center on Disabilities, which coordinates information centers nationwide (see Resources). These groups know the laws and how to help people with disabilities receive the fair treatment they deserve.

KEEPING A SENSE OF HUMOR

Tics can look goofy. They can erupt at the most inconvenient times. Being able to laugh during these situations relieves tension. Yes, tics are awful at times. But they cannot change the person inside. Tics are only one part of who someone is. Laughter helps keep TS in perspective.

"If I can get my sense of humor to take over [when tics are embarrassing], that usually helps," Mark notes. "Even though I have a warped sense of humor, it usually makes people laugh."

THINKING POSITIVELY ABOUT THE FUTURE

Kids with TS tally a varied list of achievements. Raymond excels in math and will enter a university program to be an engineer. Jake plays soccer. Brian has a flare for creative writing and acting. Caroline gets good grades and enjoys cooking. The list is endless. Every day these people prove they are more than their tics.

A small percentage of adults continue to struggle with life-altering tics. Despite TS, these individuals enter every walk of life. They become teachers, lawyers, scientists, secretaries, mechanics, doctors, and salespeople. Some say TS boosts their careers. Big-name athletes claim to benefit from the quick, coordinated

Having TS does not mean having to sacrifice the joys of artistic expression.

movements that come with TS. Artists insist that the wildness of their tics inspires rushes of creativity for colorful visions, musical themes, and fantastic story-lines. All try to make the most of their talents.

As Brian reasons, "I am proud of who I am. I might change in five or six years. My whole life story isn't written out yet. When you can be proud of yourself, you can do other things."

SOURCE NOTES

Chapter One
1. Jason Valencia, *Tourette's Syndrome: A Young Man's Poetic Journey through Childhood* (Skokie, IL: Tourette Syndrome Association, 1998), p. 2.

Chapter Two
1. Adam Seligman and John Hilkevich, eds., *Don't Think about Monkeys: Extraordinary Stories by People with Tourette Syndrome* (Duarte, CA: Hope Press, 1992), pp. 142-143.
2. Oliver Sacks, *An Anthropologist on Mars* (New York: Knopf, 1995), p. 97.
3. Leslie Packer, *Tourette Syndrome Plus: Rage Attacks: Awareness*, http://www.tourettesyndrome.net/rage_awareness.htm.
4. Ibid.

Chapter Three
1. Howard Kushner, *A Cursing Brain? The History of Tourette Syndrome* (Cambridge, MA: Harvard University Press), p. 11.
2. Daniel Weinberger, M.D., and Steven Wolf, M.D., "What Makes Tics Tick? Clues Found in Tourette Twins' Caudates," http://www.nimh.nih.gov/events/prtouter.htm; also in Thomas Hyde and Daniel Weinberger, "Tourette's Syndrome: A Model Neuropsychiatric Disorder," *JAMA*, vol. 273, no. 6 (Feb. 8, 1995), pp. 498-502.
3. "Triple Tourette's," *Science News*, vol. 137, no. 8 (Feb. 24, 1990), p. 125.

Chapter Five
1. Elaine Shimberg, *Living with Tourette Syndrome* (New York: Simon & Schuster, 1994), p. 123.
2. Quoted in "TS in the Family: Brother and Sisters Coping Together," *Tourette Syndrome Association Newsletter*, vol. 28, no. 3 (Winter 2000), p. 1.
3. Ibid., p. 1.

Chapter Six
1. Stephen Policoff, "Diseases Your Doctor May Miss," *Ladies' Home Journal*, vol. 107, no. 6 (1990), p. 105.
2. William Rubin, "Living with Tourette Syndrome: 'I Am Not My Tics,'" in *Children with Tourette Syndrome: A Parent's Guide* (Rockville, MD: Woodbine House, 1992), p. 255.
3. Quoted in "Tourette Syndrome," *Personnel Journal*, vol. 71, no. 6 (June 1992), pp. 92-93.

GLOSSARY

antibodies: substances created in the body to fight off disease

autoimmune reaction: a situation when substances in the body that are supposed to fight infection attack healthy tissue as well

basal ganglia: nerve clusters deep within the brain that play a role in smooth muscle actions and stopping and starting movement; thought to be the area involved with tics

biofeedback: a procedure that retrains the brain through exercises that monitor brain responses by computer

caudate nucleus: area within the basal ganglia portion of the brain that transmits messages from the brain to control movement

cognitive therapy: organized treatment with a therapist that retrains the brain to react differently in trouble-producing situations, reducing obsessive movements

complex tics: coordinated patterns of movements involving several muscle groups

compulsions: actions someone must perform to ease discomfort caused by certain repeated distressful thoughts or images

coprolalia: complex vocal tic that involves saying curses or socially inappropriate words

copropraxia: complex motor tic that involves making offensive gestures

dopamine: chemical, a neurotransmitter, in the brain that regulates movement and balance; excess dopamine triggers severe tics

echolalia: complex vocal tic that involves repeating the last sound, word, or phrase said by someone else

echopraxia: complex motor tic that involves imitating someone else's actions

genes: basic units of heredity present on a chromosome that create traits in the body; passed from parents to child

Human Genome (gene) Project: national research program that seeks to provide a map of genes for every trait and disease

mecamylamine: nicotine-like drug for high blood pressure that is being tested for use to reduce tics

motor tics: sudden uncontrollable movements that arise from muscles of the body

neuroleptics: common class of medications prescribed for tics that suppresses the action of dopamine, the chemical that transmits impulses between nerve cells

neurologist: medical doctor who specializes in the nervous system

neurotransmitters: chemicals in the brain that carry messages from one brain cell to another

nicotine: drug in tobacco that makes smoking addictive but can increase the manufacture of dopamine enough to shut down its production and reduce tics

norephinephrine: neurotransmitter in the brain that may influence how messages in the brain control movement

obsessions: thoughts or images that return over and over again, interfering with everyday activities

palilalia: complex vocal tic that involves repeating one's own words or sounds

pediatrician: medical doctor who specializes in caring for children and adolescents

psychiatrist: medical doctor who specializes in mental problems and who can prescribe medication

psychologist: someone trained to counsel patients with emotional or behavior problems; cannot prescribe medication

resource room: special class in school where small numbers of students receive extra attention so they can handle their schoolwork in a regular class setting

serotonin: neurotransmitter in the brain that affects emotion, balance, and thought and transmits messages involving movement

simple tics: individual repeated movements of only one body part, such as head jerking

special needs class: separate full-time classroom for students with disabilities who need adapted learning situations

stimulant: type of medication given to treat ADD that boosts the flow of brain chemicals

strep (streptococcal pharyngitis): infection that invades the body and could play a role in triggering tics

syndrome: disorder with a combination of symptoms

tardive dyskinesia: movement disorder that sometimes results from taking neuroleptics

testosterone: male hormone

tics: movements and sounds beyond a person's control

tranquilizer: type of medication that helps smooth the action of neurotransmitters

vocal tics: sudden uncontrollable movements that come from muscles controlling speech

RESOURCES

These organizations provide additional information about Tourette syndrome and related conditions. Check directory assistance for government agencies that may change locations with administrations.

Specific to Tourette Syndrome:

Tourette Syndrome Association, Inc. (TSA)

42-40 Bell Blvd., Suite 205

Bayside, New York 11361-2820

(718) 224-2999

www.tsa-usa.org

National organization for Tourette syndrome that furnishes referrals to local TSAs, physicians, and advocacy resources and offers print and video information and workshops about all aspects of Tourette syndrome. Locals run support groups and camps for families touched by TS

National Organization for Rare Disorders (NORD)
P.O. Box 8923
New Fairfield, CT 06812-8923
(800) 999-6673 for general information and ordering materials; (203) 746-6518 to speak with a representative
http://www.rarediseases.org

National organization that provides information free and for a fee about rare diseases, including Tourette syndrome, a medication assistance program for families who cannot afford drugs, and diagnostic and treatment referrals

National Institute of Neurological Disorders and Stroke
P.O. Box 13050
Silver Spring, MD 20911
(800) 352-9424
http://www.ninds.nih.gov

National organization that provides information about diseases and research programs

General Disabilities and Health Care:
American Academy of Pediatrics
141 Northwest Point Boulevard
Elk Grove Village, IL 60007-1098
(800) 433-9016
http://www.aap.org

Association headquarters for pediatricians that offers referrals, information, and publications

Association of University Centers on Disabilities Programs for Persons with Developmental Disabilities
1010 Wayne Avenue, Suite 920
Silver Spring, MD 20910
(301) 588-8252
www.aucd.org

National network with local branches that provides health care, diagnosis, referrals, and research

National Dissemination Center for Children with Disabilities
P.O. Box 1492
Washington, DC 20013
(800) 695-0285
nichcy@aed.org
http://www.nichcy.org

Public agency that provides information and referrals

Family Resource Center on Disabilities
20 East Jackson Boulevard, Room 300
Chicago, IL 60604
(800) 952-4199
(312) 939-3519 (TDD)
www.frcd.org

Nonprofit agency that provides information, referrals, and advocacy tips

MedicAlert
2323 Colorado Avenue
Turlock, CA 95382-1009
(888) 633-4298
www.medicalert.org

Company that sells bracelets and necklaces with information about illness and disability, including Tourette syndrome

Related Conditions:
Yale University Child Study Center
TS/OCD Specialty Clinic and Research Group
230 South Frontage Rd.
New Haven, CT 06520
(203) 785-5880 or (203) 785-2511
http://info.med.yale.edu/chldstdy/tsocd

University research and information source knowledgeable about TS

Obsessive-Compulsive Foundation, Inc.
676 State Street
New Haven, CT 06511
(203) 401-2070
info@ocfoundation.org
http://ocfoundation.org

National organization for information, professional referrals, local groups, and conferences concerning obsessive-compulsive disorder

CHADD (Children and Adults with Attention Deficit/Hyperactivity Disorder)
8181 Professional Place, Suite 150
Landover, MD 20785
(800) 233-4050
http://www.chadd.org

National organization for information, professional referrals, local groups, and conferences concerning ADD and ADHD

Learning Disabilities Association of America (LDA)
4156 Library Road
Pittsburgh, PA 15234-1349
(412) 341-1515
http://www.ldanatl.org

National organization for information, professional referrals, local groups, and conferences concerning learning disabilities

National Human Genome Research Institute
National Institutes of Health
Building 31, Room 4B09
31 Center Drive, MSC 2152
9000 Rockville Pike
Bethesda, MD 20892-2152
301-402-0911
http://www.genome.gov

Genetic research arm of the National Institutes of Health that supports research and distributes up-to-date information about causes and treatment of many child development issues, including Tourette syndrome. The e-mail site will lead you to the most recent results of genetic research.

Helpful Web Sites:

A Story of Tourette Syndrome
http://kidshealth.org/kid/health_problems/brain/k_tourette.html

Kidshealth has three pages for kids, teens, and parents

Pharmacological Treatment
http://www.geocites.com/Hollywood/2219/pharm.html

MedicineNet.com
http://www.medicinenet.com

Tourette Syndrome "Plus"
http://www.tourettesyndrome.net

Tourette-Syndrome.com
http://www.tourette-syndrome.com

National Institute of Mental Health
http://www.nimh.nih.gov

Government source for studies related to TS, strep infections, and other autoimmune disorders

Virtual Children's Hospital

A Digital Library of Pediatric Information

http://www.vh.org/pediatric/patient/psychiatry/prose/tourettes.html

University of Iowa virtual hospital site

FOR FURTHER READING

For Kids Who Want to Understand Tourette Syndrome

Harris, Jacqueline. *Hereditary Diseases*. New York: Twenty-First Century Books, 1993.

Landau, Elaine. *Tourette Syndrome*. Danbury, CT: Franklin Watts, 1998.

Moe, Barbara. *Coping with Tourette Syndrome and Tic Disorders*. New York: Rosen Publishing Group, 2000.

For Brothers and Sisters

Meyer, Donald. *Living with a Brother or Sister with Special Needs*. Seattle: University of Washington Press, 1996.

Meyer, Donald. *Views from Our Shoes: Growing Up with a Brother or Sister with Special Needs*. Bethesda, MD: Woodbine House, 1997

For Parents, Teachers, and Older Readers

Comings, David. *Tourette Syndrome and Human Behavior*. Duarte, CA: Hope Press, 1990.

Fowler, Rick. *The Unwelcome Companion*. Cashiers, NC: Silver Run Publications, 1996.

Haerle, Tracy, ed. *Children with Tourette Syndrome: A Parent's Guide*. Rockville, MD: Woodbine House, 1992.

Handler, Lowell. *Twitch and Shout: A Touretter's Tale*. New York: Dutton, 1998.

Kushner, Howard. *A Cursing Brain? The Histories of Tourette Syndrome*. Cambridge: Harvard University Press, 1999.

Sacks, Oliver. *The Man Who Mistook His Wife for a Hat and Other Clinical Tales*. New York: Summit Books, 1985.

Shimberg, Elaine Fantle. *Living with Tourette Syndrome*. New York: Simon & Schuster, 1994.

Wilensky, Amy. *Passing for Normal: A Memoir of Compulsion*. New York: Broadway Books, 1999.

INDEX

Page numbers in *italics* refer to illustrations.